D0668779

Great Speeches and Soliloquies from

Shakespeare Plays

Table of Contents

1. KING RICHARD THE SECOND: ACT 2, SCENE 1

John of Gaunt is near to death, and grieves over the fate of England in the hands of King Richard. At the same time, he extols the virtues of his country.

JOHN OF GAUNT

Methinks I am a prophet new-inspired,
And thus, expiring, do foretell of him.
His rash, fierce blaze of riot cannot last,
For violent fires soon burn out themselves.
Small showers last long, but sudden storms are short.
He tires betimes that spurs too fast betimes.
With eager feeding food doth choke the feeder.
Light vanity, insatiate cormorant,
Consuming means, soon preys upon itself.
This royal throne of kings, this sceptred isle,
This earth of majesty, this seat of Mars,
This other Eden, demi-paradise,
This fortress built by nature for herself
Against infection and the hand of war,
This happy breed of men, this little world,
This precious stone set in the silver sea,
Which serves it in the office of a wall,
Or as a moat defensive to a house
Against the envy of less happier lands;
This blessed plot, this earth, this realm, this England,
This nurse, this teeming womb of royal kings,
Feared by their breed and famous by their birth,
Renowned for their deeds as far from home
For Christian service and true chivalry

As is the sepulchre, in stubborn Jewry,
Of the world's ransom, blessed Mary's son;
This land of such dear souls, this dear dear land,
Dear for her reputation through the world,
Is now leased out -I die pronouncing it -
Like to a tenement or pelting farm.
England, bound in with the triumphant sea,
Whose rocky shore beats back the envious siege
Of watry Neptune, is now bound in with shame,
With inky blots and rotten parchment bonds.
That England that was wont to conquer others
Hath made a shameful conquest of itself.
Ah, would the scandal vanish with my life,
How happy then were my ensuing death!

2. KING RICHARD THE SECOND: ACT 3, SCENE 2

Richard, facing defeat and death, reflects upon the fate of kings, and realises that they, too, are merely frail mortals.

KING RICHARD

Of comfort no man speak.
Let's talk of graves, of worms and epitaphs,
Make dust our paper, and with rainy eyes
Write sorrow on the bosom of the earth.

Let's choose executors and talk of wills -
And yet not so, for what can we bequeath
Save our deposed bodies to the ground?
Our lands, our lives, and all are Bolingbroke's;
And nothing can we call our own but death,
And that small model of the barren earth
Which serves as paste and cover to our bones
(Sitting) For God's sake, let us sit upon the ground,
And tell sad stories of the death of kings --
How some have been deposed, some slain in war,
Some haunted by the ghosts they have deposed,
Some poisoned by their wives, some sleeping killed,
All murdered. For within the hollow crown
That rounds the mortal temples of a king
Keeps Death his court; and there the antic sits,
Scoffing his state and grinning at his pomp,
Allowing him a breath, a little scene,
To monarchize, be feared, and kill with looks.
Infusing him with self and vain conceit,
As if this flesh which walls about our life
Were brass impregnable; and humoured thus,
Comes at the last, and with a little pin
Bores through his castle wall; and farewell, king.
Cover your heads, and mock not flesh and blood
With solemn reverence. Throw away respect,
Tradition, form, and ceremonious duty,
For you have but mistook me all this while.
I live with bread, like you; feel want,
Taste grief, need friends.
Subjected thus,
How can you say to me I am a king?

3. KING HENRY THE FOURTH, PART 1: ACT 2, SCENE 3

Lady Percy, the dashing rebel Hotspur's young and loving wife, demands to know why his sleep is troubled by violent images of war and death.

LADY PERCY

O my good lord, why are you thus alone?
For what offence have I this fortnight been
A banished woman from my Harry's bed?
Tell me, sweet lord, what ist that takes from thee
Thy stomach, pleasure, and thy golden sleep?
Why dost thou bend thine eyes upon the earth,
And start so often when thou sittst alone?
Why hast thou lost the fresh blood in thy cheeks,
And given my treasures and my rights of thee
To thick-eyed musing and cursed melancholy?
In thy faint slumbers I by thee have watched,
And heard thee murmur tales of iron wars,
Speak terms of manage to thy bounding steed,
Cry Courage! To the field! And thou hast talked
Of sallies and retires, of trenches, tents,
Of palisadoes, frontiers, parapets,
Of basilisks, of cannon, culverin,
Of prisoners ransomed, and of soldiers slain,
And ail the currents of a heady fight.
Thy spirit within thee hath been so at war,
And thus hath so bestirred thee in thy sleep,
That beads of sweat have stood upon thy brow

Like bubbles in a late-disturbed stream;
And in thy face strange motions have appeared,
Such as we see when men restrain their breath
On some great sudden hest. O, what portents are these?
Some heavy business hath my lord in hand,
And I must know it, else he loves me not.

4. KING HENRY THE FOURTH, PART 2: ACT 3, SCENE 1

King Henry, troubled by rebellion and, more deeply, by his own earlier usurpation of the throne, laments his inability to sleep, and envies the poor their careless slumbers.

KING HENRY

How many thousand of my poorest subjects
Are at this hour asleep? O sleep, O gentle sleep,
Natures soft nurse, how have I frighted thee,
That thou no more wilt weigh my eyelids down
And steep my senses in forgetfulness?
Why rather, sleep, liest thou in smoky cribs,
Upon uneasy pallets stretching thee,
And hushed with buzzing night-flies to thy slumber,
Than in the perfumed chambers of the great,
Under the canopies of costly state,

And lulled with sound of sweetest melody?
O thou dull god, why li'st thou with the vile
In loathsome beds, and leavst the kingly couch
A watch-case, or a common larum-bell?
Wilt thou upon the high and giddy mast
Seal up the ship-boy's eyes, and rock his brains
In cradle of the rude imperious surge,
And in the visitation of the winds,
Who take the ruffian billows by the top,
Curling their monstrous heads，and hanging them
With deafening clamour in the slippery shrouds,
That, with the hurly, death itself awakes?
Canst thou, O partial sleep, give thy repose
To the wet sea-boy in an hour so rude,
And in the calmest and most stillest night,
With all appliances and means to boot,
Deny it to a king? Then happy low, lie down.
Uneasy lies the head that wears a crown.

5. KING HENRY THE FOURTH, PART 2: ACT 4, SCENE 5

Prince Harry, watching by his sick father's bedside, begins to understand the burden of kingship. Then, mistakenly believing that his father has died in his sleep, he places the crown on his own head and vows to fulfill his destiny as monarch.

PRINCE HARRY

Why doth the crown lie there upon his pillow,
Being so troublesome a bedfellow?
O polished perturbation! Golden care!
That keepst the ports of slumber open wide
To many a watchful night! -Sleep with it now!
Yet not so sound, and half so deeply sweet,
As he whose brow with homely biggen bound
Snores out the watch of night. O majesty!
When thou dost pinch thy bearer, thou dost sit
Like a rich armour worn in heat of day,
That scaldst with safety. By his gages of breath
There lies a downy feather which stirs not.
Did he suspire, that light and weightless down
Perforce must move. -My gracious lord, my father!-
This sleep is sound indeed. This is a sleep
That from this golden rigol hath divorced
So many English kings.-Thy due from me
Is tears and heavy sorrows of the blood,
Which nature, love, and filial tenderness
Shall, O dear father, pay thee plenteously.
My due from thee is this imperial crown,
Which, as immediate from thy place and blood,
Derives itself to me.
(He puts the crown on his head)
Where it sits,
Which God shall guard; and put the world's whole strength
Into one giant arm, it shall not force
This lineal honour from me. This from thee
Will I to mine leave as tis left to me. (Exits)

6. KING HENRY THE FOURTH, PART 2: ACT 4, SCENE 3

Falstaff, the fat-bellied lover of brothel and tavern, has received permission from the puritanical Prince John to leave the battlefield, victory over the rebels having been secured. Falstaff praises the virtues of sherry-sack in promoting manly courage.

FALSTAFF

Good faith, this same young sober blooded boy doth not love me, nor a man cannot make him laugh. But that's no marvel, he drinks no wine. There's never none of these demure boys come to any proof; for thin drink doth so overcool their blood, and making many fish meals, that they fall into a kind of male greensickness; and then, when they marry, they get wenches. They are generally fools and cowards -- which some of us should be too, but for inflammation. A good sherry-sack hath a two-fold operation in it. It ascends me into the brain, dries me there all the foolish and dull and crudy vapours which environ it, makes it apprehensive, quick, forgetive, full of nimble, fiery, and delectable shapes, which, delivered o'er to the voice, the tongue, which is the birth, becomes excellent wit. The second property of your excellent sherry is the warming of the blood, which, before cold and settled, left the liver white and pale, which is the badge of pusillanimity and cowardice. But the sherry warms it, and makes it course from the inwards to the parts extremes; it illuminateth the face, which, as a beacon, gives warning to all the rest of this little kingdom, man, to arm; and then the vital commoners and inland petty spirits muster me all to their captain, the heart; who, great and puffed up with this retinue, doth any deed of courage. And this valour comes of sherry. So that skill in the weapon is nothing without sack, for that sets it a-work; and learning a mere hoard of gold kept by a devil, till sack commences it and sets it in act and use. Hereof comes it that Prince Harry is valiant; for the cold blood he did naturally inherit of his father he hath, like lean, sterile, and bare land, manured, husbanded, and tilled, with excellent endeavour of drinking good, and good store of fertile sherry, that he is become very hot and valiant. If I had a thousand sons, the first human principle would teach them should be to forswear thin potations, and to addict themselves to sack.

7. KING HENRY THE FIFTH: ACT 2, SCENE 3

Mistress Quickly, hostess of the tavern, tells of the death Falstaff. Broken by the new King's rejection of him, the old sinner (Mistress Quickly believes) must surely have re pen and earned a place in heaven ...

HOSTESS

Nay, sure he's not in hell. He's in Arthur's bosom, if ever m went to Arthur's bosom. A made a finer end, and went away it had been any christom child. A parted ev'n just between twelve and one, ev'n at the turning o'th tide -- for after I saw him fumble with the sheets, and play with flowers, and smile upon his fingers' end, I knew there was but one way. For his nose was as sharp as a pen, and a babbled of green fields. How now, Sir John? Quoth I. What, man! Be o good cheer. So a cried out, God, God, God, three or four times. Now I, to comfort him, bid him a should not think of God; I hoped there was no need to trouble himself with any such thought yet. So a bade me lay more clothes on his feet. I put my hand into the bed and felt them, and they were as cold as any stone. Then I felt to his knees, and so upard and upard, and all was as cold as any stone.

8. KING HENRY THE FIFTH: THE PROLOGUE

The Chorus invites the audience to use its imagination in helping to bring the great events of the play to life.

CHORUS

O for a Muse of fire, that would ascend
The brightest heaven of invention:
A kingdom for a stage, princes to act,
And monarchs to behold the swelling scene.
Then should the warlike Harry, like himself,

Assume the port of Mars, and at his heels,
Leashed in like hounds, should famine, sword, and fire
Crouch for employment. But pardon, gentles all,
The flat unraised spirits that hath dared
On this unworthy scaffold to bring forth
So great an object. Can this cock-pit hold
The vasty fields of France? Or may we cram
Within this wooden O the very casques
That did affright the air at Agincourt?
O pardon: since a crooked figure may
Attest in little place a million,
And let us, ciphers to this great account,
On your imaginary forces work.
Suppose within the girdle of these walls
Are now confined two mighty monarchies,
Whose high upreared and abutting fronts
The perilous narrow ocean parts asunder.
Piece out our imperfections with your thoughts:
Into a thousand parts divide one man,
And make imaginary puissance.
Think, when we talk of horses, that you see them,
Printing their proud hoofs i'th' receiving earth;
For tis your thoughts that now must deck our kings,
Carry them here and there, jumping o'er times,
Turning th' accomplishment of many years
Into an hourglass - for the which supply,
Admit me Chorus to this history,
Who Prologue-like your humble patience pray
Gently to hear, kindly to judge, our play.

9. KING HENRY THE FIFTH: ACT 3, SCENE 1

The King, sensing that the impetus of his army's attack Harfleur is flagging, urges the soldiers on to one last decisive effort.

KING HENRY

Once more unto the breach, dear friends, once more,
Or close the wall up with our English dead.
In peace there's nothing so becomes a man
As modest stillness and humility,
But when the blast of war blows in our ears,
Then imitate the action of the tiger.
Stiffen the sinews, conjure up the blood,
Disguise fair nature with hard-favoured rage.
Then lend the eye a terrible aspect,
Let it pry through the portage of the head
Like the brass cannon, let the brow o'erwhelm it
As fearfully as doth a galled rock
O'erhang and jutty his confounded base,
Swilled with the wild and wasteful ocean.
Now set the teeth and stretch the nostril wide,
Hold hard the breath, and bend up every spirit
To his full height. On, on, you noblest English,
Whose blood is fet from fathers of war-proof,
Fathers that like so many Alexanders
Have in these parts from morn till even fought,
And sheathed their swords for lack of argument.
Dishonour not your mothers; now attest
That those whom you called fathers did beget you.
Be copy now to men of grosser blood,

And teach them how to war. And you, good yeomen,
Whose limbs were made in England, show us here
The mettle of your pasture; let us swear
That you are worth your breeding - which I doubt not,
For there is none of you so mean and base
That hath not noble lustre in your eyes.
I see you stand like greyhounds in the slips,
Straining upon the start. The game's afoot.
Follow your spirit, and upon this charge
Cry, God for Harry! England and Saint George!
(Alarum, and chambers go off. Exeunt)

10. KING HENRY THE FIFTH: ACT 4, SCENE 1

It is the eve of Agincourt, and the King, in disguise, has discovered that his men hold him responsible for their next day's fate....

KING HENRY

Upon the King.
Let us our lives, our souls, our debts, our care-full wives,
Our children, and our sins, Lay on the King.
We must bear all. O hard condition,
Twin-born with greatness, subject to the breath
Of every fool whose sense no more can feel
But his own wringing. What infinite heart's ease

Must kings neglect that private men enjoy?
And what have kings that privates have not too,
Save ceremony, save general ceremony?
And what art thou, thou idol Ceremony?
What kind of god art thou, that sufferst more
Of mortal griefs than do thy worshippers?
What are thy rents? What are thy comings-in?
O Ceremony, show me but thy worth!
What is thy soul of adoration?
Art thou aught else but place, degree, and form,
Creating awe and fear in other men?
Wherein thou art less happy, being feared,
Than they in fearing.
What drinkst thou oft, instead of homage sweet,
But poisoned flattery? O be sick, great greatness,
And bid thy Ceremony give thee cure!
Thinkst thou the fiery fever will go out
With titles blown from adulation?
Will it give place to fLexure and low bending?
Canst thou, when thou commandst the beggar's knee,
Command the health of it? No, thou proud dream
That playst so subtly with a king's repose;
I am a king that find thee, and I know
Tis not the balm, the sceptre, and the ball,
The sword, the mace, the crown imperial,
The intertissued robe of gold and pearl,
The farced title running fore the king,
The throne he sits on, nor the tide of pomp
That beats upon the high shore of this world-
No, not all these, thrice-gorgeous ceremony,
Not all these, laid in bed majestical,
Can sleep so soundly as the wretched slave

Who, with a body filled and vacant mind,
Gets him to rest, crammed with distressful bread;
Never sees horrid night, the child of hell,
But like a lackey from the rise to set
Sweats in the eye of Phoebus, and all night
Sleeps in Elysium, next day, after dawn
Doth rise and help Hyperion to his horse,
And follows so the ever-running year
With profitable labour to his grave.
And, but for ceremony, such a wretch,
Winding up days with toil and nights with sleep,
Had the forehand and vantage of a king.
The slave, a member of the country's peace,
Enjoys it; but in gross brain little wots
What watch the King keeps to maintain the peace,
Whose hours the peasant best advantages.

11. KING HENRY THE FIFTH: ACT 4, SCENE 3

Dawn breaks on the day of the battle of Agincourt. The King, hearing Warwick wish for reinforcements, tells his men victory will be all the more glorious if it is achieved against the odds.

KING HENRY

If we are marked to die, we arc enough

To do our country loss; and if to live,
The fewer men, the greater share of honour.
God's will, I pray thee wish not one man more.
By Jove, I am not covetous for gold,
Nor care I who doth feed upon my cost;
It ernes me not if men my garments wear;
Such outward things dwell not in my desires.
But if it be a sin to covet honour
I am the most offending soul alive.
No, faith, my coz, wish not a man from England.
God's peace, I would not lose so great an honour
As one man more methinks would share from me
For the best hope I have. O do not wish one more.
Rather proclaim it presently through my host
That he which hath no stomach to this fight,
Let him depart. His passport shall be made
And crowns for convoy put into his purse.
We would not die in that man's company
That fears his fellowship to die with us.
This day is called the Feast of Crispian.
He that outlives this day and comes safe home
Will stand a-tiptoe when this day is named
And rouse him at the name of Crispian.
He that shall see this day and live t'old age
Will yearly on the vigil feast his neighbours
And say, Tomorrow is Saint Crispian.
Then will he strip his sleeve and show his scars
And say, These wounds I had on Crispin's day.
Old men forget; yet all shall be forgot,
But he'll remember, with advantages,
What feats he did that day. Then shall our names,
Familiar in his mouth as household words -

Harry the King, Bedford and Exeter,
Warwick and Talbot, Salisbury and Gloucester -
Be in their flowing cups freshly remembered.
This story shall the good man teach his son,
And Crispin Crispian shall ne'er go by
From this day to the ending of the world
But we in it shall be remembered.   .
We few, we happy few, we band of brothers.
For he today that sheds his blood with me
Shall be my brother; be he neer so vile,
This day shall gentle his condition.
And gentlemen in England now abed
Shall think themselves accursed they were not here,
And hold their manhoods cheap whiles any speaks
That fought with us upon Saint Crispin's day

12. KING HENRY THE SIXTH, PART 3: ACT 1, SCENE 4

The Wars of the Roses are in progress. Margaret, the Lancastrian Queen, captures her sworn enemy, the Duke of York.

MARGARET

Brave warriors, Clifford and Northumberland,
Come make him stand upon this molehill here,

That raught at mountains with outstretched arms,
Yet parted but the shadow with his hand.
What, was it you that would be England's king?
Wast you that revelle'd in our parliament,
And made a preachment of your high descent?
Where are your mess of sons, to back you now?
The wanton Edward, and the lusty George?
And where's that valiant crook-back prodigy,
Dicky, your boy, that with his grumbling voice
Was wont to cheer his dad in mutinies?
Or with the rest, where is your darling Rutland?
Look York, I stain'd this napkin with his blood
That valiant Clifford, with his rapier's point,
Made issue from the bosom of the boy;
And if thine eyes can water for his death,
I give thee this to dry thy cheeks withal.
Alas poor York, but that I hate thee deadly,
I should lament thy miserable state.
I prithee grieve, to make me merry, York.
What, hath thy fiery heart so parch'd thine entrails,
That not a tear can fall for Rutland's death?
Why art thou patient man, thou shouldst be mad;
And I, to make thee mad, do mock thee thus.
Stamp, rave, and fret, that 1 may sing and dance.
Thou wouldst be feed, I see, to make me sport:
York cannot speak, unless he wear a crown.
A crown for York; and lords, bow low to him.
Hold you his hands, whilst I do set it on
(Putting a paper crown on his head)
Ay marry sir, now looks he like a king.
Ay, this is he that took King Henry's chair,
And this is he was his adopted heir.

But how is it that the great Plantagenet
Is crowned so soon, and broke his solemn oath?
As I bethink me, you should not be king,
Till our King Henry had shook hands with death.
And will you pale your head in Henry's glory,
And rob his temples of the diadem,
Now in his life, against your holy oath?
O tis a fault too too unpardonable.
Off with the crown; and with the crown, his head;
And whilst we breathe, take time to do him dead.

13. KING RICHARD THE THIRD: ACT 1, SCENE 1

The deformed Richard of Gloucester proclaims his determination to set his brother Clarence and King Edward in deadly hate against each other.

RICHARD OF GLOUCESTER

Now is the winter of our discontent
Made glorious summer by this son of York;
And all the clouds that loured upon our house
In the deep bosom of the ocean buried.
Now are our brows bound with victorious wreaths,
Our bruised arms hung up for monuments,
Our stern alarums changed to merry meetings,
Our dreadful marches to delightful measures.

Grim-visaged war hath smoothed his wrinkled front,
And now - instead of mounting barbed steeds
To fright the souls of fearful adversaries -
He capers nimbly in a lady's chamber
To the lascivious pleasing of a lute.
But I, that am not shaped for sportive tricks
Nor made to court an amorous looking glass;
I, that am rudely stamped, and want love's majesty
To strut before a wanton ambling nymph;
I, that am curtailed of this fair proportion,
Cheated of feature by dissembling Nature,
Deformed, unfinished, sent before my time
Into this breathing world scarce half made up --
And that so lamely and unfashionable
That dogs bark at me as I halt by them --
Why, I, in this weak piping time of peace
Have no delight to pass away the time,
Unless to spy my shadow in the sun
And descant on mine own deformity.
And therefore, since I cannot prove a lover
To entertain these fair well-spoken days,
I am determined to prove a villain
And hate the idle pleasures of these days.
Plots have I laid, inductions dangerous,
By drunken prophecies, libels and dreams,
To set my brother Clarence and the King
In deadly hate the one against the other.
And if King Edward be as true and just
As I am subtle, false, and treacherous,
This day should Clarence closely be mewed up
About a prophecy that says that G
Of Edward's heirs the murderer shall be.

14. KING RICHARD THE THIRD: ACT 1, SCENE 4

The Duke of Clarence, unaware of his brother Richard's evil intentions towards him, has been imprisoned in the Tower and has dreamed t of drowning and damnation.

CLARENCE

O, I have pass'd a miserable night,
So full of ugly sights, of ghastly dreams,
That, as I am a Christian faithful man,
I would not spend another such a night
Though twere to buy a world of happy days,
So full of dismal terror was the time.
Methought that I had broken from the Tower,
And was embark'd to cross to Burgundy;
And in my company my brother Gloucester,
Who from my cabin tempted me to walk
Upon the hatches: thence we look'd toward England,
And cited up a thousand heavy times,
During the wars of York and Lancaster,
That had befall'n us. As we pac'd along
Upon the giddy footing of the hatches,
Methought that Gloucester stumbled; and, in falling,
Struck me, that thought to stay him, overboard,
Into the tumbling billows of the main.
Lord, Lord! methought what pain it was to drown:
What dreadful noise of water in mine ears!
What sights of ugly death within mine eyes!

Methought I saw a thousand fearful wracks;
A thousand men that fishes gnaw'd upon;
Wedges of gold, great anchors, heaps of pearl,
Inestimable stones, unvalu'd jewels,
All scatter'd in the bottom of the sea.
Some lay in dead men's skulls; and in those holes
Where eyes did once inhabit, there were crept,
As twere in scorn of eyes, reflecting gems,
That woo'd the slimy bottom of the deep,
And mock'd the dead bones that lay scatter'd by.
I had such leisure in the time of death
To gaze upon these secrets of the deep -
Or thought I had; and often did I strive
To yield the ghost; but still the envious flood
Stopt in my soul, and would not let it forth
To find the empty, vast, and wandering air;
But smotherd it within my panting bulk,
Which almost burst to belch it in the sea.
And yet my dream was lengthen'd after life;
O! then began the tempest to ray soul.
I pass'd, methought, the melancholy flood,
With that grim ferryman which poets write of,
Unto the kingdom of perpetual night.
The first that there did greet my stranger soul,
Was my great father-in-law, renowned Warwick;
Who cried aloud, What scourge for perjury
Can this dark monarchy afford false Clarence?
And so he vanish'd: then came wandering by
A shadow like an angel, with bright hair
Dabbled in blood; and he shriek'd out aloud,
Clarence is come, - false, fleeting, perjur'd Clarence,
That stabb'd me in the field by Tewksbury;-

Seize on him! Furies, take him unto torment.
With that, methought a legion of foul fiends
Environ'd me, and howled in mine ears
Such hideous cries, that with the very noise
I trembling wak'd, and, for a season after,
Could not believe but that I was in hell,
Such terrible impression made my dream.
O Brakenbury! I have done these things
That now give evidence against my soul,
For Edward's sake; and see how he requites me.
O God! if my deep prayers cannot appease thee,
But thou wilt be aveng'd on my misdeeds,
Yet execute thy wrath on me alone:
O! spare my guiltless wife and my poor children.
I pray thee, gentle keeper, stay by me;
My soul is heavy, and I fain would sleep.

15. THE MERCHANT OF VENICE: ACT 4, SCENE 1

Portia, disguised as a young Doctor of Law, explains to Shylock why he cannot claim his pound of flesh, and begins by reflecting on the virtues of mercy.

PORTIA

The quality of mercy is not strained.
It droppeth as the gentle rain from heaven

Upon the place beneath. It is twice blest:
It blesseth him that gives, and him that takes.
Tis mightiest in the mightiest. It becomes
The throned monarch better than his crown.
His sceptre shows the force of temporal power,
The attribute to awe and majesty,
Wherein doth sit the dread and fear of kings;
But mercy is above this sceptred sway.
It is enthroned in the hearts of kings;
It is an attribute to God himself,
And earthly power doth then show likest Gods
When mercy seasons justice. Therefore, Jew,
Though justice be thy plea, consider this:
That in the course of justice none of us
Should see salvation. We do pray for mercy,
And that same prayer doth teach us ail to render
The deeds of mercy. I have spoke thus much
To mitigate the justice of thy plea,
Which if thou follow, this strict court of Venice
Must needs give sentence gainst the merchant there

16. AS YOU LIKE IT: ACT 2, SCENE 7

Jaques, the cynical wit, imagines life as a play in seven acts with each of us an actor who must play many parts......

JAQUES

All the worid's a stage,
And all the men and women merely players.
They have their exits and their entrances,
And one man in his time plays many parts,
His acts being seven ages. At first the infant,
Mewling and puking in the nurse's arms.
Then the whining schoolboy with his satchel
And shining morning face, creeping like snail
Unwillingly to school. And then the lover,
Sighing like furnace, with a woeful ballad Made
to his mistress' eyebrow. Then, a soldier,
Full of strange oaths, and bearded like the pard,
Jealous in honour, sudden, and quick in quarrel,
Seeking the bubble reputation
Even in the cannon's mouth. And then the justice,
In fair round belly with good capon lined,
With eyes severe and beard of formal cut,

Full of wise saws and modem instances;
And so he plays his part. The sixth age shifts
Into the lean and slippered pantaloon,
With spectacles on nose and pouch on side,
His youthful hose, well saved, a world too wide
For his shrunk shank, and his big, manly voice,
Turning again toward childish treble, pipes
And whistles in his sound. Last scene of all,
That ends this strange, eventful history,
Is second childishness and mere oblivion,
Sans teeth, sans eyes, sans taste, sans everything.

17. A MIDSUMMER NIGHTS DREAM: ACT 2, SCENE 1

Titania, Queen of the Fairies, is at odds with her husband Oberon over possession of an Indian Pageboy, and feelingly evokes the chaos wrought in the human world by their discord.

TITANIA

These are the forgeries of jealousy,
And never since the middle summer's spring
Met we on hill, in dale, forest, or mead,
By paved fountain or by rushy brook,
Or in the beachM margin of the sea
To dance our ringlets to the whistling wind,
But with thy brawls thou hast disturbed our sport.
Therefore the winds, piping to us in vain,
As in revenge have sucked up from the sea
Contagious fogs which, falling in the land,
Hath every pelting river made so proud
That they have overborne their continents.
The ox hath therefore stretched his yoke in vain,
The ploughman lost his sweat, and the green corn
Hath rotted ere his youth attained a beard.
The fold stands empty in the drowned field,
And crows are fatted with the murrain flock.
The nine men's morris is filled up with mud,
And the quaint mazes in the wanton green
For lack of tread are undistinguishable.

The human mortals want their winter cheer:
No night is now with hymn or carol blessed.
Therefore the moon, the governess of floods,
Pale in her anger washes all the air,
That rheumatic diseases do abound;
And thorough this distemperature we see
The seasons alter: hoary-headed frosts
Fall in the fresh lap of the crimson rose,
And on old Hiems thin and icy crown
An odorous chaplet of sweet summer buds
Is, as in mock'ry, set. The spring, the summer,
The childing autumn, angry winter change
Their wonted liveries, and the mazed world
By their increase now knows not which is which;
And this same progeny of evils comes
From our debate, from our dissension.
We are their parents and original.

18. THE TAMING OF THE SHREW: ACT 5, SCENE 2

Katherine has yielded authority to her new husband, Petruchio, controlling her former shrewish temper. She argues that the husband must be lord.

KATHERINE

Fie, fie, unknit that threat'ning, unkind brow,
And dart not scornful glances from those eyes
To wound thy lord, thy king, thy governor.
It blots thy beauty as frosts do bite the meads,
Confounds thy fame as whirlwinds shake fair buds,
And in no sense is meet or amiable.
A woman moved is like a fountain troubled,
Muddy, ill-seeming, thick, bereft of beauty,
And while it is so, none so dry or thirsty
Will deign to sip or touch one drop of it.
Thy husband is thy lord, thy life, thy keeper,
Thy head, thy sovereign, one that cares for thee,
And for thy maintenance commits his body
To painful labour both by sea and land,
To watch the night in storms, the day in cold,
Whilst thou liest warm at home, secure and safe,
And craves no other tribute at thy hands
But love, fair looks, and true obedience,
Too little payment for so great a debt.
Such duty as the subject owes the prince,
Even such a woman oweth to her husband,
And when she is froward, peevish, sullen, sour,
And not obedient to his honest will,
What is she but a foul contending rebel,
And graceless traitor to her loving lord?
I am ashamed that women are so simple
To offer war where they should kneel for peace,
Or seek for rule, supremacy, and sway
When they are bound to serve, love, and obey.
Why are our bodies soft, and weak, and smooth,
Unapt to toil and trouble in the world,
But that our soft conditions and our hearts

Should well agree with our external parts?

Come, come, you froward and unable works,
My mind hath been as big as one of yours,
My heart as great, my reason haply more,
To bandy word for word and frown for frown;
But now I see our lances are but straws,
Our strength as weak, our weakness past compare,
That seeming to be most which we indeed least are.
Then vail your stomachs, for it is no boot.
And place your hands below your husband's foot,
In token of which duty, if he please,
My hand is ready, may it do him ease.

19. TROILUS AND CRESSIDA: ACT 5, SCENE 2

Troilus has been watching his beloved Cressida in the arms of Diomedes. He struggles to understand this treachery, vows to turn his love to vengeful hate.

TROILUS

This, she? No, this is Diomed's Cressida.
If beauty have a soul, this is not she.
If souls guide vows, if vows be sanctimonies,
If sanctimony be the god's delight,
If there be rule in unity itself,

This is not she. O madness of discourse,
That cause sets up with and against thyself!
Bifold authority, where reason can revolt
Without perdidon, and loss assume all reason
Without revolt! This is and is not Cressida.
Within my soul there doth conduce a fight
Of this strange nature, that a thing inseparate
Divides more wider than the sky and earth,
And yet the spacious breadth of this division
Admits to orifex for a point as subtle
As Ariachne's broken woof to enter.
Instance, O instance, strong as Pluto's gates:
Cressida is mine, tied with the bonds of heaven.
Instance, O instance, strong as heaven itself:
The bonds of heaven are slipped, dissolved, and loosed;
And with another knot, five-finger-tied,
The fractions of her faith, orts of her love,
The fragments, scraps, the bits and greasy relics
Of her o'er-eaten faith, are bound to Diomed.
Hark, Greek: as much as I do Cressida love,
So much by weight hate I her Diomed.
That sleeve is mine that he'll bear in his helm.
Were it a casque composed by Vulcan's skill,
My sword should bite it. Not the dreadful spout
Which shipmen do the hurricano call,
Constringed in mass by the almighty sun,
Shall dizzy with more clamour Neptune's ear
In his descent, than shall my prompted sword
Falling on Diomed.

20. TROILUS AND CRESSIDA: ACT 5, SCENE 3

Ulysses seeks to persuade the sullen Achilles to rejoin the fight against the Trojans, reminding him that honorable deeds are soon forgotten, and that he must renew his reputation by fresh feats of arms.

ULYSSES

Time hath, my lord,
A wallet at his back, wherein he puts
Alms for oblivion, a great-sized monster
Of ingratitudes. Those scraps are good deeds past,
Which are devoured as fast as they are made,
Forgot as soon as done. Perseverance, dear my lord,
Keeps honour bright. To have done is to hang
Quite out of fashion, like a rusty mail
In monumental mock'ry. Take the instant way,
For honour travels in a strait so narrow,
Where one but goes abreast. Keep then the path,
For emulation hath a thousand sons
That one by one pursue: if you give way,
or hedge aside from the direct forthright,
Like to an entered tide they all rush by
And leave you hindmost;
Or, like a gallant horse fall'n in first rank,
Lie there for pavement to the abject rear,
O'errun and trampled on. Then what they do in present,
Though less than yours in past, must o'ertop yours.
For Time is like a fashionable host,

That slightly shakes his parting guest by th'hand
And, with his arms outstretched as he would fly,
Grasps in the comer. Welcome ever smiles,
And farewell goes out sighing. O let not virtue seek
Remuneration for the thing it was;
For beauty, wit,
High birth, vigor of bone, desert in service,
Love, friendship, charity, are subjects all
To envious and calumniating time.
One touch of nature makes the whole world kin -
That all with one consent praise new-born gauds,
Though they are made and moulded of things past,
And give to dust that is a little gilt
More laud than gilt o'er-dusted.
The present eye praises the present object.
Then marvel not, thou great and complete man,
That all the Greeks begin to worship Ajax,
Since things in motion sooner catch the eye
Than what not stirs. The cry went once on the tee,
And still it might, and yet it may again,
If thou wouldst not entomb thyself alive
And case thy reputation in thy tent,
Whose glorious deeds but in these fields of late
Made emulous missions mongst the gods themselves,
And drove great Mars to faction.

21. THE TWO NOBLE KINSMEN: ACT 2, SCENE 4

The Jailer's daughter, fifteen years old, is infatuated with the noble prisoner Palamon, and looks for some way of winning his love.

JAILER'S DAUGHTER

Why should I love this gentleman? Tis odds
He never will affect me. I am base,
My father the mean keeper of his prison,
And he a prince. To marry him is hopeless,
To be his whore is witless. Out upon t,
What pushes are we wenches driven to
When fifteen once has found us? First, I saw him;
I, seeing, thought he was a goodly man;
He has as much to please a woman in him -
If he pleases to bestow it so -as ever
These eyes yet looked on. Next, I pitied him,
And so would any young wench, o my conscience,
That ever dreamed or vowed her maidenhead
To a young handsome man. Then, I loved him,
Extremely loved him, infinitely loved him -
And yet he had a cousin fair as he, too.
But in my heart was Falamon, and there,
Lord, what a coil he keeps! To hear him
Sing in an evening, what a heaven it is!
And yet his songs are sad ones. Fairer spoken
Was never gentleman. When I come in
To bring him water in a morning, first

He bows his noble body, then salutes me, thus:
Fair, gentle maid, good morrow. May thy goodness
Get thee a happy husband. Once he kissed me -
I loved my lips the better ten days after.
Would he would do so every day! He grieves much,
And me as much to see his misery.
What should I do to make him know I love him?
For I would fain enjoy him. Say 1 ventured
To set him free? What says the law then?
Thus much
For law or kindred! I will do it.
And this night: ere tomorrow he shall love me.

22. JULIUS CAESAR: ACT 2, SCENE 1

It is night time in Brutus' garden. Brutus has agreed to the plot to assassinate Caesar. His wife Portia comes to out her troubled husband and discover what is ailing him.

PORTIA

My lord,
You've ungently, Brutus,
Stole from my bed; and yesternight at supper
You suddenly arose, and walked about
Musing and sighing, with our arms across;

And when I asked you what the matter was,
You stared upon me with ungentle looks.
I urged you further; then you scratched your head,
And too impatiently stamped with your foot.
Yet I insisted; yet you answered not.
But with an angry wafture of your hand
Gave sign for me to leave you. So I did,
Fearing to strengthen that impatience
Which seemed too much enkindled, and withal
Hoping it was but an effect of humour,
Which sometime hath his hour with every man.
It will not let you eat, nor talk, nor sleep;
And could it work so much upon your shape
As it hath much prevailed on your condition,
I should not know you Brutus. Dear my lord,
Make me acquainted with your cause of grief.
Brutus is wise, and were he not in health
He would embrace the means to come by it.
Is Brutus sick? And is it physical
To walk unbraced and suck up the humours
Of the dank morning? What, is Brutus sick?
And will he steal out of his wholesome bed
To dare the vile contagion of the night,
And tempt the rheumy and unpurged air
To add unto his sickness? No, my Brutus,
You have some sick offence within your mind,
Which by the right and virtue of my place
I ought to know of. (Kneeling) And upon my knees,
I charm you by my once-commended beauty.
By all your vows of love, and that great vow
Which did incorporate and make us one,
That you unfold to me, your self, your half,

Why you arc heavy, and what men tonight
Have had resort to you - for here have been
Some six or seven, who did hide their faces
Even from darkness. (She rises)
Within the bond of marriage, tell me, Brutus,
Is it excepted I should know no secrets
That appertain to you? Am I your self
But as it were in sort or limitation?
To keep with you at meals, comfort your bed,
And talk to you sometimes? Dwell I but in the suburbs
Of your good pleasure? If it be no more,
Portia is Brutus's harlot, not his wife.

23. JULIUS CAESAR: ACT 3, SCENE 1

**Caesar has been killed by the conspirators. Mark
Antony, Caesar's mast devoted disciple, vows to avenge
his death.**

ANTONY

O pardon me, thou bleeding piece of earth,
That I am meek and gentle with these butchers.
Thou art the ruins of the noblest man
That ever lived in the tide of times.
Woe to the hand that shed this costly blood!
Over thy wounds now do I prophesy -
Which like dumb mouths do ope their ruby lips

To beg the voice and utterance of my tongue -
A curse shall light upon the limbs of men;
Domestic fury and fierce civil strife
Shall cumber all the parts of Italy;
Blood and destruction shall be so in use,
And dreadful objects so familiar,
That mothers shall but smile when they behold
Their infants quartered with the hands of war,
All pity choked with custom of fell deeds;
And Caesar's spirit, ranging for revenge,
With Ate by his side come hot from hell,
Shall in these confines with a monarch's voice
Cry havoc! and let slip the dogs of war,
That this foul deed shall smell above the earth
With carrion men, groaning for burial.

24. JULIUS CAESAR: ACT 3, SCENE 2

Antony has been allowed by Brutus to speak at Caesar's funeral, and seizes this opportunity to work on sympathies of the crowd.

ANTONY

Friends, Romans, countrymen, lend me your ears.
I come to bury Caesar, not to praise him.
The evil that men do lives after them;
The good is oft interred with their bones.

So let it be with Caesar. The noble Brutus
Hath told you Caesar was ambitious.
If it were so, it was a grievous fault,
And grievously hath Caesar answered it.
Here, under leave of Brutus and the rest -
For Brutus is an honorable man,
So are they all, all honorable men -
Come I to speak in Caesar's funeral.
He was my friend, faithful and just to me.
But Brutus says he was ambitious,
And Brutus is an honorable man.
He hath brought many captives home to Rome,
Whose ransoms did the general coffers fill.
Did this in Caesar seem ambitious?
When that the poor have cried, Caesar hath wept.
Ambition should be made of sterner stuff.
Yet Brutus says he was ambitious,
And Brutus is an honorable man.
You all did see that on the Lupercal
I thrice presented him a kingly crown,
Which he did thrice refuse. Was this ambition?
Yet Brutus says he was ambitious,
And sure he is an honorable man.
I speak not to disprove what Brutus spoke,
But here I am to speak what I do know.
You all did love him once, not without cause.
What cause withholds you then to mourn for him?
O judgment, thou art fled to brutish beasts,
And men have lost their reason!
(He weeps)
Bear with me.
My heart is in the coffin there with Caesar,

And I must pause tiD it come back to me.

25. ROMEO AND JULIET: ACT 1, SCENE 3

Juliet's old Nurse and Lady Capulet are talking about Juliet's childhood. and the Nurse is led into fond reminiscence.

NURSE

Faith. I can tell her age unto an hour.
Even or odd. of all days in the year.
Come Lammas Eve at night shall she be fourteen.
Susan and she - God rest all Christian souls!-
Were of an age: well. Susan is with God;
She was too good for me-but. as I said,
On Lammas Eve at night shall he be fourteen;
That shall be, marry; I remember it well.
'Tis since the earthquake now eleven years;
And she was wean'd, -I never shall forget it,   —
Of all the days of the year, upon that day:
For I had then laid wormwood to my dug,
Sitting in the sun under the dove-house wall;
My lord and you were then at Mantua:
Nay, I do bear a brain: - But, as I said,
When it did taste the wormwood on the nipple
Of my dug, and felt it bitter, pretty fool,
To see it tetchy, and fall out with the dug!
Shake, quoth the dove-house; 'twas no need, I trow,
To bid me trudge.
And since that time it is eleven years;

For then she could stand high lone; nay, by the rood.
She could have run and waddled all about;
For even the day before, she broke her brow;
And then my husband, -- God be with his soul!
A was a merry man, - took up the child:
Yea, quoth he, dost thou fall upon thy face?
Thou wilt fall backward when thou hast more wit;
Wilt thou not, Jule? And, by my holidame,
The pretty wretch left crying and said Ay:
To see, now, how a jest shall come about!
I warrant, an I should live a thousand years,
I never shall forget it: Wilt thou not, Jule? quoth he;
And, pretty fool, it stinted, and said Ay.
And to think it should leave crying, and say Ay:
And yet, I warrant, it had upon its brow
A bump as big as a young cockerel's stone;
A parlous knock; and it cried bitterly.
Yea, quoth my husband, fall'st upon thy face?
Thou wilt fall backward when thou com'st to age;
Wilt thou not, Jule? It stinted, and said Ay.

26. ROMEO AND JULIET: ACT 2, SCENE 2

Romeo has stolen into the Capulets' garden, seeking
Juliet whom he met at the nasked ball. She is not aware
of his presence.

ROMEO

But soft, what light through yonder window breaks?
It is the east, and Juliet is the sun.
Arise, fair sun, and kill the envious moon,
Who is already sick and pale with grief
That thou, her maid, art far more fair than she.
Be not her maid, since she is envious.
Her vestal livery is but sick and green,
And none but fools do wear it; cast it off.
(Enter Juliet aloft)
It is my lady! O, it is my love!
O that she knew she were!
She speaks, yet she says nothing. What of that?
Her eye discourses; I will answer it.
I am too bold. Tis not to me she speaks.
Two of the fairest stars in all the heaven,
Having some business, do entreat her eyes
To twinkle in their spheres till they return.
What if her eyes were there, they in her head?-
The brightness of her cheek would shame those stars
As daylight doth a lamp; her eye in heaven
Would through the airy region stream so bright
That birds would sing and think it were not night.
See how she leans her cheek upon her hand!
O, that I were a glove upon that hand,
That I might touch that cheek!
JULIET
Ay me.
ROMEO (aside)
She speaks.
O, speak again, bright angel; for thou art

As glorious to this night, being o'er my head,
As is a winged messenger of heaven
Unto the white upturned wond'ring eyes
Of mortals that fall back to gaze on him
When he bestrides the lazy-passing clouds
And sails upon the bosom of the air.

27. ROMEO AND JULIET: ACT 3, SCENE 2

The lovers have married in secret, and Juliet awaits Romeo, impatient for the onset of night.

JULIET

Gallop apace, you fieiy-footed steeds,
Towards Phoebus' lodging! Such a waggoner
As Phaeton would whip you to the west
And bring in cloudy night immediately.
Spread thy close curtain, love-performing night,
That runaways eyes may wink, and Romeo
Leap to these arms untalked of and unseen.
Lovers can see to do their amorous rites
By their own beauties; or, if love be blind,
It best agrees with night. Come, civil night,
Thou sober-suited matron all in black,
And learn me how to lose a winning match
Played for a pair of stainless maidenhoods.

Hood my unmanned blood, bating in my cheeks,
With thy black mantle till strange love grown bold
Think true love acted simple modesty.
Come, night; come, Romeo; come, thou day in night;
For thou wilt lie upon the wings of night
Whiter than new snow on a raven's back.
Come, gentle night; come, loving, black-browed night;
Give me my Romeo, and when I shall die
Take him and cut him out in little stars,
And he will make the face of heaven so fine
That all the world will be in love with night
And pay no worship to the garish sun.
O, I have bought the mansion of a love
But not possessed it, and though I am sold,
Not yet enjoyed. So tedious is this day
As is the night before some festival
To an impatient child that hath new robes
And may not wear them.

28. HAMLET: ACT 1, SCENE 2

Hamlet's father has died suddenly. The young man's rage and horror at his mother's swift remarriage emerge in full when he is alone.

HAMLET

O that this too too solid flesh would melt,
Thaw, and resolve itself into a dew,
Or that the Everlasting had not fixed
His canon gainst self-slaughter! O God, O God,
How weary, stale,flat, and unprofitable
Seem to me all the uses of this world!
Fie on't, ah fie, fie! Tis an unweeded garden
That grows to seed; things rank and gross in nature
Possess it merely. That it should come to this -
But two months dead - nay, not so much, not two-
So excellent a king, that was to this
Hyperion to a satyr, so loving to my mother
That he might not beteem the winds of heaven
Visit her face too roughly! Heaven and earth,
Must I remember? Why, she would hang on him
As if increase of appetite had grown
By what it fed on, and yet within a month -
Let me not think on't; frailty, thy name is woman -
A little month, or ere those shoes were old
With which she followed my poor father's body,
Like Niobe, all tears, why she, even she -
O God, a beast that wants disclosure of reason
Would have mourned longer! - married with mine uncle,
My father's brother, but no more like my father
Than I to Hercules. Within a month,
Ere yet the salt of most unrighteous tears
Had left the flushing of her galled eyes,
She married. O most wicked speed, to post
With such dexterity to incestuous sheets!
It is not, nor it cannot come to good.
But break, my heart, for I must hold my tongue.

29. HAMLET: ACT 1, SCENE 3

The ageing politician Polonius offers some worldly advice to his son Laertes, who is leaving for France.

POLONIUS

Yet here, Laertes? Aboard, aboard, for shame!
The wind sits in the shoulder of your sail,
And you are stayed for. There - my blessing with thee,
And these few precepts in thy memory
See thou character. Give thy thoughts no tongue,
Nor any unproportioned thought his act.
Be thou familiar, but by no means vulgar.
The friends thou hast, and their adoption tried,
Grapple them to thy soul with hoops of steel,
But do not dull thy palm with entertainment
Of each new-hatched unfledged comrade. Beware
Of entrance to a quarrel, but being in,
Bear't that th'opposed may beware of thee.
Give every man thine ear but few thy voice.
Take each man's censure, but reserve thy judgement.
Costly thy habit as thy purse can buy,
But not expressed in fancy; rich not gaudy;
For the apparel oft proclaims the man,
And they in France of the best rank and station
Are of all most select and generous, chief in that.
Neither a borrower nor a lender be,
For loan oft loses both itself and friend,
And borrowing dulls the edge of husbandry.

This above all - to thine own self be true,
And it must follow, as the night the day,
Thou canst not then be false to any man.
Farewell - my blessing season this in thee.

30. HAMLET: ACT 3, SCENE 1

Hamlet wonders aloud at man's ability to endure the pain and injustice of this life.

HAMLET

To be, or not to be; that is the question;
Whether tis nobler in the mind to suffer
The slings and arrows of outrageous fortune,
Or To take arms against a sea of troubles.
And, by opposing, end them. To die, to sleep -
No more - and by a sleep to say we end
The heartache and the thousand natural shocks
That flesh is heir to - tis a consummation
Devoutly to be wished. To die, to sleep -
To sleep, perchance to dream. Ay, there's the rub,
For in that sleep of death what dreams may come
When we have shuffled off this mortal coil
Must give us pause. There's the respect
That makes calamity of so long life,
For who would bear the whips and scorns of time,

Th'oppressor's wrong, the proud man's contumely,
The pangs of disprized love, the law's delay,
The insolence of office, and the spurns
That patient merit of th'unworthy takes,
When he himself might his quietus make
With a bare bodkin? Who would these fardels bear,
To grunt and sweat under a weary life,
But that the dread of something after death,
The undiscovered country from whose bourn
No traveller returns, puzzles the will,
And makes us rather bear those ills we have
Than fly to others that we know not of?
Thus conscience does make cowards of us all,
And thus the native hue of resolution
Is sicklied o'er with the pale cast of thought,
And enterprises of great pitch and moment
With this regard their currents turn awry,
And lose the name of action.

31. HAMLET: ACT 3, SCENE 1

Ophelia, terrified by Hamlet's violent and cruel behaviour, laments what she sees as his madness and grieves over ending of their love.

OPHELIA

O, what a noble mind is here o'erthrown!
The courtier's, soldier's, scholar's eye, tongue, sword,
Th'expectancy and rose of the fair state,
The glass of fashion and the mould of form,
Th' observed of all observers, quite, quite, down!
And I, of ladies most deject and wretched,
That sucked the honey of his music vows,
Now see that noble and most sovereign reason
Like sweet bells jangled out of tune and harsh;
That unmatched form and feature of blown youth
Blasted with ecstasy. O woe is me,
T' have seen what I have seen, see what I see!

32. HAMLET: ACT 3, SCENE 3

Claudius, who has murdered Hamlet's father to become King, fears retribution and prays in vain for God's forgiveness.

KING CLAUDIUS

O, my offence is rank! It smells to heaven.
It hath the primal eldest curse upon't,
A brothers murder. Pray can I not.
Though inclination be as sharp as will,
My stronger guilt defeats my strong intent,
And like a man to double business bound

I stand in pause where I shall first begin,
And both neglect. What if this cursed hand
Were thicker than itself with brother's blood,
Is there not rain enough in the sweet heavens
To wash it white as snow? Where to serves mercy
But to confront the visage of offence?
And what's in prayer but this twofold force,
To be forestalled, ere we come to fall,
Or pardoned, being down? Then I'll look up.
My fault is past. But O, what form of prayer
Can serve my turn? Forgive me my foul murder?
That cannot be, since I am still possessed
Of those effects for which I did the murder -
My crown, mine own ambition, and my queen.
May one be pardoned and retain th' offence?
In the corrupted currents of this world
Offence's gilded hand may shove by justice,
And oft tis seen the wicked prize itself
Buys out the law. But tis not so above.
There is no shuffling, there the action lies
In his true nature, and we ourselves compelled
Even to the teeth and forehead of our faults
To give in evidence. What then? What rests?
Try what repentance can. What can it not?
Yet what can it when one cannot repent?
O wretched state, O bosom black as death!
O limed soul that, struggling to be free,
Art more engaged! Help, angels! Make assay.
Bow, stubborn knees; and heart with strings of steel,
Be soft as sinews of the new-born babe.
All may be well.
(He kneels)

33. HAMLET: ACT 4, SCENE 7

Queen Gertrude tells Laertes of his sister Ophelia's death by drowning.

QUEEN GERTRUDE

There is a willow grows aslant a brook
That shows his hoar leaves in the glassy stream.
Therewith fantastic garlands did she make
Of crow-flowers, nettles, daisies, and long purples,
That liberal shepherds give a grosser name,
But our cold maids do dead men's fingers call them.
There on the pendent boughs her coronet weeds
Clambering to hang, an envious sliver broke,
When down the weedy trophies and herself
Fell in the weeping brook. Her clothes spread wide,
And mermaid-like a while they bore her up;
Which time she chanted snatches of old tunes,
As one incapable of her own distress,
Or like a creature native and endued
Unto that element. But long it could not be
Till that her garments, heavy with their drink,
Pulled the poor wretch from her melodious lay
To muddy death.

34. OTHELLO: ACT 1, SCENE 3

Othello answers the charge that he has abducted Desdemona by telling the story of their courtship.

OTHELLO

Her father loved me, oft invited me,
Still questioned me the story of my life
From year to year, the battles, sieges, fortunes
That I have passed.
I ran it through even from my boyish days
To th' very moment that he bade me tell it,
Wherein I spoke of most disastrous chances,
Of moving accidents by flood and field,
Of hair-breadth scapes i'th' imminent deadly breach,
Of being taken by the insolent foe
And sold to slavery, of my redemption thence,
And portance in my traveller's history,
Wherein of antres vast and deserts idle,
Rough quarries, rocks, and hills whose heads touch heaven,
It was my hint to speak. Such was my process,
And of the cannibals that each other eat,
The Anthropophagi, and men whose heads
Do grow beneath their shoulders. These things to hear
Would Desdemona seriously incline,
But still the house affairs would draw her thence,
Which ever as she could with haste dispatch
She'd come again, and with a greedy ear
Devour up my discourse; which I observing.

Took once a pliant hour, and found good means
To draw from her a prayer of earnest heart
That I would all my pilgrimage dilate,
Whereof by parcels she had something heard,
But not intentively. I did consent,
And often did beguile her of her tears
When I did speak of some distressful stroke
That my youth suffered. My story being done,
She gave me for my pains a world of kisses.
She swore in faith Twas strange, twas passing strange,
Twas pitiful, twas wondrous pitiful.
She wished she had not heard it, yet she wished
That heaven had made her such a man. She thanked me,
And bade me, if I had a friend that loved her,
I should but teach him how to tell my story,
And that would woo her. Upon this hint I spake.
She loved me for the dangers I had passed,
And I loved her that she did pity them.
This only is the witchcraft I have used.
(Enter Desdemona, Iago, and attendants)

35. OTHELLO: ACT 5, SCENE 2

Othello has been tricked into a mad jealousy and has killed beloved Desdemona. Seizing his sword, he is forced o acknowledge that military prowess cannot help him now, as he laments his terrible crime against the innocent Desdemona.

OTHELLO

Behold, 1 have a weapon;
A better never did itself sustain
Upon a soldier's thigh. I have seen the day
That, with this little arm and this good sword,
I have made my way through more impediments
Than twenty times your stop. But O, vain boast!
Who can control his fate? Tis not so now.
Be not afraid, though you do see me weaponed.   .
Here is my journey's end, here is my butt
And very sea-mark of my utmost sail.
Do you go back dismayed? Tis a lost fear.
Man but a rush against Othello's breast
And he retires. Where should Othello go?
(To Desdemona) Now, how dost thou look now? O ill-starred wench,
Pale as thy smock! When we shall meet at count
This look of thine will hurl my soul from heaven,
And fiends will snatch at it.
(He touches her)
Cold, cold, my girl,

Even like thy chastity. O cursed, cursed slave!
Whip me, ye devils,
From the possession of this heavenly sight.
Blow me about in winds, roast me in sulphur,
Wash me in steep-down gulfs of liquid fire!
O Desdemon! Dead Desdemon! Dead! O! O!

36. KING LEAR: ACT 1, SCENE 2

Edmund, bastard son of Gloucester, vigorously proclaims his intention of displacing his legitimate brother Edgar as their father's heir.

EDMUND

Thou, Nature, art my goddess. To thy law
My services are bound. Wherefore should I
Stand in the plague of custom and permit
The curiosity of nations to deprive me
For that I am some twelve or fourteen moonshines
Lag of a brother? Why bastard? Wherefore base,
When my dimensions are as well compact,
My mind as generous, and my shape as true
As honest madam's issue? Why brand they us
With base, with baseness, bastardy - base, base -
Who in the lusty stealth of nature take
More composition and fierce quality

Than doth within a dull, stale, tired bed
Go to th' creating a whole tribe of fops
Got tween sleep and wake? Well then,
Legitimate Edgar, I must have your land.
Our father's love is to the bastard Edmund
As to th' legitimate. Fine word, legitimate.
Well, my legitimate, if this letter speed
And my invention thrive, Edmund the base
Shall top th' legitimate. I grow, I prosper.
Now gods, stand up for bastards!

37. MACBETH: ACT 1, SCENE 5

Lady Macbeth is reading a letter from her husband in which he describes the witches' prophecy that he will become King. She plans to spur him on to this great prize.

LADY MACBETH (reading)

They met me in the day of success, and I have learned by the perfectst report they have more in them than mortal knowledge. When I burned in desire to question them further, they made themselves air, into which they vanished. Whiles I stood rapt in the wonder of it came missives from the King, who all-hailed j me, Thane of Cawdor, by which title before these weird sisters saluted me, and referred me to the coming on of time with Hail, King that shalt be! This have I thought good to deliver thee, my dearest partner of greatness, that thou mightst not lose the dues of rejoicing by being ignorant of what greatness is promised thee. Lay it to thy heart, and farewell.

Glamis thou art, and Cawdor, and shalt be
What thou art promised. Yet do I fear thy nature.
It is too full o' th' milk of human kindness
To catch the nearest way. Thou wouldst be great,
Art not without ambition, but without
The illness should attend it. What thou wouldst highly,
That wouldst thou holily; wouldst not play false,
And yet wouldst wrongly win. Thoudst have, great Glamis,
That which cries Thus thou must do if thou have it,
And that which rather thou dost fear to do
Than wishest should be undone. Hie thee hither,
That I may pour my spirits in thine ear
And chastise with the valour of my tongue
All that impedes thee from the golden round
Which fate and metaphysical aid doth seem
To have thee crowned withal.

38. MACBETH: ACT 1, SCENE 5

Lady Macbeth has learnt that King Duncan will stay in her castle that night. She invokes the powers of darkness to give her strength in carrying out her murderous plan.

LADY MACBETH

The raven himself is hoarse
That croaks the fatal entrance of Duncan
Under my battlements. Come, you spirits
That tend on mortal thoughts, unsex me here,
And fill me from the crown to the toe top-full
Of direst cruelty. Make thick my blood,
Stop up th' access and passage to remorse,
That no compunctious visitings of nature
Shake my fell purpose, nor keep peace between
Th' effect and it. Come to my woman's breasts,
And take my milk for gall, you murd'ring ministers.
Wherever in your sightless substances
You wait on nature's mischief. Come, thick night,
And pall thee in the dunnest smoke of hell,
That my keen knife see not the wound it makes,
Nor heaven peep through the blanket of the dark
To cry Hold, Hold!

39. MACBETH: ACT 1, SCENE 7

Macbeth, now resolved to kill the King, fears that the performance of such a terrible deed will inevitably be discovered and punished.

MACBETH

If it were done when tis done, then twere will
It were done quickly. If the assassination
Could trammel up the consequence, and catch
With his surcease success: that but this blow
Might be the be-all and the end-all, here,
But here upon this bank and shoal of time,
We'd jump the life to come. But in these cases
We still have judgement here, that we but teach
Bloody instructions which, being taught, return
To plague th' Inventor. This even-handed justice
Commends th' ingredience of our poisoned chalice
To our own lips. He's here in double trust:
First, as I am his kinsman and his subject,
Strong both against the deed; then, as his host,
Who should against his murderer shut the door,
Not bear the knife myself. Besides, this Duncan
Hath borne his faculties so meek, hath been
So clear in his great office, that his virtues
Will plead like angels, trumpet-tongued against
The deep damnation of his taking-off,
And pity, like a naked new-born babe,
Striding the blast, or heaven's cherubin, horsed

Upon the sightless couriers o' the air,
Shall blow the horrid deed in every eye
That tears shall drown the wind. I have no spur
To prick the sides of my intent, but only
Vaulting ambition which oerleaps itself
And falls on th' other.

40 MACBETH: ACT 2, SCENE 1

**Macbeth is waiting in tense anticipation for the signal
from his wife to carry out the murder of Duncan.**

MACBETH

Is this a dagger which I see before me,
The handle toward my hand? Come, let me clutch thee.
I have thee not, and yet I see thee still.
Art thou not, fatal vision, sensible
To feeling as to sight? Or art thou but
A dagger of the mind, a false creation
Proceeding from the heat-oppressed brain?
I see thee yet, in form as palpable .
As this which now I draw.
Thou marshallst me the way that I was going,
And such an instrument I was to use.
Mine eyes are made the fools o' th' other senses,
Or else worth all the rest. I see thee still,

And on thy blade and dudgeon gouts of blood
Which was not so before. There's no such thing.
It is the bloody business which informs
Thus to mine eyes. Now o'er the one half-world
Nature seems dead, and wicked dreams abuse
The curtained sleep. Witchcraft celebrates
Pale Hecate's offerings, and withered murder,
Alarumed by his sentinel the wolf,
Whose howl's his watch, thus with his stealthy pace,
With Tarquin's ravishing strides, towards his design
Moves like a ghost. Thou sure and firm-set earth,
Hear not my steps which way they walk, for fear
Thy very stones prate of my whereabout,
And take the present horror from the time,
Which now suits with it. Whiles I threat, he lives.
Words to the heat of deeds too cold breath gives.
(A bell rings)
I go, and it is done, The bell invites me.
Hear it not, Duncan; for it is a knell
That summons thee to heaven, or to hell.

41. MACBETH: ACT 5, SCENE 5

Macbeth's castle is under siege by the forces of Malcolm, and he knows his end is near. Now he is told of his wife's death.

MACBETH

She should have died hereafter.
There would have been a time for such a word.
Tomorrow, and tomorrow, and tomorrow
Creeps in this petty pace from day to day
To the last syllable of recorded time,
And all our yesterdays have lighted fools
The way to dusty death. Out, out, brief candle.
Life's but a walking shadow, a poor player
That struts and frets his hour upon the stage,
And then is heard no more. It is a tale
Told by an idiot, full of sound and fury,
Signifying nothing.

42. ANTONY AND CLEOPATRA: ACT 2, SCENE 2

Enobarbus describes the occasion on which Antony first saw Cleopatra and was bewitched by her beauty.

ENOBARBUS

The barge she sat in, like a burnished throne
Burned on the water. The poop was beaten gold;
Purple the sails, and so perfumed that
The winds were love-sick with them. The oars were silver,
Which to the tune of flutes kept stroke, and made

The water which they beat to follow faster,
As amorous of their strokes. For her own person,
It beggared all description. She did lie
In her pavilion - cloth of gold, of tissue -
O'er-picturing that Venus where we see
The fancy outwork nature. On each side her
Stood pretty dimpled boys, like smiling Cupids,
With divers-coloured fans whose wind did seem
To glow the delicate cheeks which they did cool,
And what they undid did.
Her gentlewomen, like the Nereides,
So many mermaids, tended her i' th' eyes,
And made their bends adornings. At the helm
A seeming mermaid steers. The silken tackle
Swell with the touches of those flower-soft hands
That yarely frame the office. From the barge
A strange invisible perfume hits the sense
Of the adjacent wharfs. The city cast
Her people out upon her, and Antony,
Enthroned i' th' market-place, did sit alone,
Whistling to the air, which but for vacancy
Had gone to gaze on Cleopatra too,
And made a gap in nature.
Upon her landing Antony sent to her,
Invited her to supper. She replied
It should be better he became her guest;
Which she entreated. Our courteous Antony,
Whom ne'er the word of No woman heard speak,
Being barbered ten times o'er, goes to the feast,
And for his ordinary pays his heart
For what his eyes eat only.
I saw her once

Hop forty paces through the public street,
And having lost her breath, she spoke and panted,
That she did make defect perfection,
And breathless, pour breath forth.
Age cannot wither her, nor custom stale
Her infinite variety. Other women cloy
The appetites they feed, but she makes hungry
Where most she satisfies. For vilest things
Become themselves in her, that the holy priests
Bless her when she is riggish.

43. ANTONY AND CLEOPATRA: ACT 1, SCENE 5

Antony has been called away to Rome, and in his absence Cleopatra lovingly imagines what he might be doing at that moment.......

CLEOPATRA

Charmian!
'O'
Give me to drink mandragora.
That I might sleep out this great gap of time
My Antony is away.
O, Charmian,
Where thinkst thou he is now? Slands he or sits he?
Or does he walk? Or is he on his horse?

O happy horse, to bear the weight of Antony!
Do bravely, horse, for wotst thou whom thou movst?-
The demi-Atlas of this earth, the arm
And burgonet of men? He's speaking now,
Or murmuring Where's my serpent of old Nile?-
For so he calls me. Now I feed myself
With most delicious poison. Think on me,
That am with Phoebus' amorous pinches black,
And wrinkled deep in time. Broad-fronted Caesar,
When thou wast here above the ground I was
A morsel for a monarch, and great Pompey
Would stand and make his eyes grow in my brow.
There would he anchor his aspect, and die
With looking on his life.
Who's born that day
When I forget to send to Antony,
Shall die a beggar. Ink and paper, Charmian.
He shall have every day a several greeting,
Or I'll unpeople Egypt.

44. ANTONY AND CLEOPATRA: ACT 4, SCENE 15

Antony dies; Cleopatra, acknowledging that she is but a woman for all her great titles, looks forward to her own death in a world that has lost all meaning.

CLEOPATRA

Noblest of men, woot die?
Hast thou no care of me, shall I abide
In this dull world, which in thy absence is
No better than a sty? O, see, my women:
The crown o' the earth doth melt.
(Antony dies)
My lord?
O, wither'd is the garland of the war,
The soldier's pole is fall'n: young boys and girls
Are level now with men: the odds is gone.
And there is nothing left remarkable
Beneath the visiting moon.
(Faints)
CLEOPATRA (recovering from a faint)
No more but e'en a woman, and commanded
By such poor passion as the maid that milks
And does the meanest chores. It were for me
To throw my sceptre at the injurious gods,
To tell them that this world did equal theirs
Till they had stol'n our jewel. All's but naught.
Patience is sottish, and impatience does
Become a dog that's mad. Then is it sin
To rush into the secret house of death
Ere death dare come to us? How do you, women?
What, what, good cheer! Why, how now, Charmian?
My noble girls! Ah, women, women! Look,
Our lamp is spent, it's out. Good sirs, take heart;
We'll bury him, and then what's brave, what's noble,
Let's do it after the high Roman fashion,
And make death proud to take us. Come, away.

This case of that huge spirit now is cold.
Ah women, women! Come, we have no friend
But resolution, and the briefest end.
(Exeunt, those above bearing off Antony's body)

45. THE TEMPEST: ACT 4, SCENE 1

**Prospero now brings these revels to a close and reflects
on the transience of life itself.**

PROSPERO

Our revels now are ended. These our actors,
As I foretold you, were all spirits, and
Are melted into air, into thin air,
And like the baseless fabric of this vision
The cloud-capped towers, the gorgeous palaces,
The solemn temples, the great globe itself,
Yea, all which it inherit, shall dissolve,
And like this insubstantial pageant faded
Leave not a rack behind. We are such stuff
As dreams are made of; and our little life
Is rounded with a sleep.

THE END

CPSIA information can be obtained
at www.ICGtesting.com
Printed in the USA
LVHW022159140820
663222LV00012B/871